IMAGES
of America

CHEROKEE
COUNTY

SOUTH CAROLINA

Cherokee County is the first publication to display this photograph of Capt. Michael Gaffney, reportedly the only photograph that exists of him. Gaffney was an immigrant from Ireland who moved into the Upstate wilderness. He founded a tavern that later brought about the settlement of Gaffney. Captain Gaffney married Mary "Polly" Smith of Smith's Ford on the Broad River, and a number of their descendants live in Cherokee County today.

2

IMAGES
of America

CHEROKEE
COUNTY
SOUTH CAROLINA

Cherokee Historical and Preservation Society, Inc.

ARCADIA
PUBLISHING

Published by Arcadia Publishing
Charleston, South Carolina

Library of Congress Catalog Card Number: 2002115945

For all general information contact Arcadia Publishing at:
Telephone 843-853-2070
Fax 843-853-0044
E-mail sales@arcadiapublishing.com
For customer service and orders:
Toll-Free 1-888-313-2665

Visit us on the Internet at www.arcadiapublishing.com

Contents

ACKNOWLEDGMENTS

Cherokee County is the culmination of support and dedication to this project by the Cherokee County History Museum and Arts Center and the membership of the Cherokee Historical and Preservation Society (CHAPS). Additionally, photographic materials and descriptive information has been graciously contributed by numerous citizens, descendants, families, historians, newspapers, and organizations.

On October 19, 2001, CHAPS member and historian Dean Ross delivered to photographer Jim Compton a never-before-seen and only recently rumored photograph of Capt. Michael Gaffney, whose colonial tavern initiated development of what is now known as Cherokee County. Ross, a direct descendant of Captain Gaffney, contributed the photograph for the specific purpose of inclusion in this publication. Of all the images compiled here, this photograph finally gives us a very notable portrait of the man who chose, for his own reasons, to settle here. Thank you Dean, for making this historical photograph a significant addition to *Cherokee County*.

The compilation of much of this publication is due solely to the efforts of Charles Farriss, a longtime CHAPS member and current member of the CHAPS Board of Directors; Ann Farriss, a longtime CHAPS member; and Jane Waters, interim director of the Cherokee County History Museum and Arts Center and current vice president of the CHAPS Board of Directors. Charles, Ann, and Jane have given countless hours and un untiring effort to the completion of *Cherokee County*. We are truly grateful for their abundant contributions.

Many citizens and organizations have also played an important role in contributing photographs and information. We would like to extend our most sincere appreciation and gratitude, in particular, to Cody Sossamon, editor of *The Gaffney Ledger*; Tommy Martin, editor of *The Cherokee Chronicle*; Jim Compton, photographer; Rodger Painter, photographer; Bobby Moss, professor and author; and Charles Copeland, CHAPS member and local historian.

If you contributed time, information, descriptions, and/or photographs, thank you for your invaluable assistance. We are sincerely appreciative of your dedication to preserving and presenting this pictorial history of Cherokee County.

Cherokee Historical and Preservation Society, Inc.

CHAPS officers are Charles Copeland, president; Jane Waters, vice president; Sara Setzer, secretary; Ron Farley, treasurer; Charles Farriss, board member.

INTRODUCTION

Settlers, attracted by mineral springs, began to move into the area now known as Cherokee County in the 1750s. They found that the friendly Congaree, Catawba, and Cherokee Indian tribes had already settled close by and were sharing this area for hunting.

Michael Gaffney, born in Granard, Ireland in 1775, immigrated to America in 1797, and arrived in New York and remained there for a couple of years before moving to Charleston, South Carolina. Gaffney, in search of a more healthy and fertile land, journeyed to this area and established a homestead here in 1804. He married Mary "Polly" Smith of the Smith's Ford family. They built a tavern and lodging house for travelers at what soon became known as "Gaffney's Cross Roads." This location was selected because of two major roads—one from the mountains of North Carolina to Charleston and the north-south route from Charlotte into Georgia.

In 1808, South Carolina governor Charles Pinckney commissioned Michael Gaffney as a captain and authorized him to form a military company, anticipating problems with Britain. In 1814 during the War of 1812, Captain Gaffney and his company were mustered into the U.S. Army. For 14 months, they were stationed near Charleston in defense of the coastline where the British were raiding. After the peace treaty, Captain Gaffney returned here and acquired and successfully operated several plantations. He died on September 6, 1854.

In 1836, several businessmen united to erect a brick resort to be called Limestone Springs Hotel. Four stories tall with long porches across each level, it quickly became the "Sarasota of the South." Many retirement homes were built and a large dance pavilion was constructed, bringing fame to the May Day celebrations. A mile-long horse racing course was built for "bloodied horses" and a $3,400 purse was among those offered. In their turn, bicycle and automobile races were also held. The hotel failed in 1845 and was purchased for the purpose of becoming a female high school. After numerous restructurings the site became known as Limestone College. Part of the college's present administration building is one of the few remaining structures from the earliest times.

In 1860, secessionist feelings began running high. When conflict began in 1861 men rushed to join one of the many local troops, but the county itself escaped actual fighting. The local iron and lead mines contributed to the cause, and Limestone Springs High School students were active in knitting and sewing for the soldiers. In 1864, Confederate deserters and Union sympathizers raided the northern areas of what would become Cherokee County. Then, in 1865, Union forces passed through pursuing Jefferson Davis just before his capture. Fourteen hundred men actually served in the Confederate services and 300 died; about 200 men returned with various disabilities.

Economic woes began to take their toll after the war. Most veterans either farmed or moved away to more prosperous areas. A railroad had been established between Columbia and Spartanburg before the war, but in 1872, the Piedmont Air Line Railroad began to run trains from Charlotte to Atlanta. Stark's Folly or Black's Station, soon to be called "Blacksburg," was also established that year. The Black brothers and their families played a major role in building Blacksburg. One of the three brothers, Thomas, showed the railroad how to grade one side of Whitaker Mountain into a suitable crossing of Broad River. The railroad then built a depot at the center of the triangle formed by the three homes of the Black brothers and named it Black's Station. In 1876, the small community was incorporated as Black's Station. In 1872, the area known as Gaffney's Old Field became known simply as "Gaffney City." The coming of the railroad in 1873 began to strengthen local commerce. In 1882, the Cherokee Falls Manufacturing Company was built on the old iron works site. Gaffney Manufacturing Company was founded in 1892 and established a cotton market that brought in additional mills that have been the foundation for this region's economy until recently.

After a bitter political fight in 1897 Cherokee County was formed in South Carolina's Upstate from parts of York, Union, and Spartanburg Counties. Gaffney was chosen as its seat of government. Several new names for the county were considered, including Limestone Springs; however, "Cherokee" won the day in honor of the Native American tribe.

Today Cherokee County is attempting to restore some of its many historical sites, but rapid change is threatening and much our our heritage has already been destroyed. The local Cherokee Historical and Preservation Society (CHAPS) is now in the midst of fund-raising to build a county history museum and arts center. This facility's mission is to ensure that preservation of our important past and an understanding of our inherited legacy is passed on to future generations of our region and our nation.

This pictorial history represents a small but significant snapshot of the people and times of Cherokee County. We sincerely hope that you enjoy it!

This c. 1920 renovation of the Michael Gaffney home was built around the original log cabin built by Michael for his family in 1804. The home was on the corner of Granard Street and Baker Boulevard in Gaffney. The back portion of the home included the original cabin of Michael Gaffney.

One

EARLY TIMES

Two unidentified men pose in front of a *c.* 1920 hunting cabin in Cherokee County. Originally a family home, the structure was later used as a hunting cabin.

Mrs. C.C. Kirby tends her flower gardens at her home on East Frederick Street in Gaffney. Mr. Kirby ran a market on North Limestone Street in the downtown business district. (Photo courtesy of Rodger Painter.)

One of the young Painter family members poses for a snapshot. The Painter family is one of the oldest families in Cherokee County. (Photo courtesy of Rodger Painter.)

Mr. C.K. Barnhill from the Draytonville community in Gaffney grinds cornmeal on his farm. The picture reveals some country ingenuity: an old tractor is used to run the mill. (Photo courtesy of Rodger Painter.)

This *c.* 1940 country "jot-em-down" store, in Thicketty Station, Gaffney, was a welcome site on the long road home. Rural stores provided for every day goods between the weekly shopping trips. Since grocery shopping was a once-a-week task, as housewives thought of items they needed, they would "jot em down" on a grocery list. Small country stores would carry simple items like bread, milk, eggs, meats, and gas for the conveniences of residents. (Photo courtesy of James Goforth.)

James Messer, in his 90s, cuts "kindling," which is used to start fires for winter warmth and cooking. He uses a handsaw and proves that you are never too old to contribute to the family needs. Messer was named "father of the year" by the *Gaffney Ledger*. (Photo courtesy of Rodger Painter.)

14

The old trade lot was located along the railroad tracks in Gaffney between Robinson and Depot Street. Farmers brought their bales of cotton to be sold to the local textile mills. Cotton brokers and farmers would settle on a fair price here.

This unidentified farmer, cotton broker, and trusty mules are on their way to the cotton sale.

Jim Jefferies, left, and Walton Lipscomb, right, are out for a "spin" on their horse-drawn buggy.

Mr. Roland Mathis, an early 1900s Cherokee County farmer, prepares for a day's hard work with his two mules.

The Tank Branch Garden Club members prepare for spring planting at the South Granard and South Logan Streets garden in Gaffney.

E.C. McArthur was born in Gaffney on March 7, 1882. He became a leading farmer, auto dealer, and a pioneer promoter of the formation of soil conservation districts. He later helped establish an association of soil conservation district supervisors, and was elected the first president of the newly formed National Association of Soil Conservation Districts. He also served as the first president of the State of South Carolina Soil and Water Conservation Districts.

Mr. Albert Davidson and his grandson are photographed at his blacksmith shop on Lincoln Street in Gaffney. Davidson's blacksmith shop and his quality of work were well known in the Gaffney area. (Photo courtesy of Rodger Painter.)

Mr. Walker Smith of Ridge Road in Gaffney draws water from his well. Pure, cool, refreshing water was drawn daily from wells like this and were a common site in Cherokee County. Although such wells are gone, well buckets are a rare find in antique shops. This well has the date of 1817 carved in the wood. (Photo courtesy of Rodger Painter.)

A binder pulled by three mules meant long days in the fields. This photograph was taken c. 1910 in rural Cherokee County.

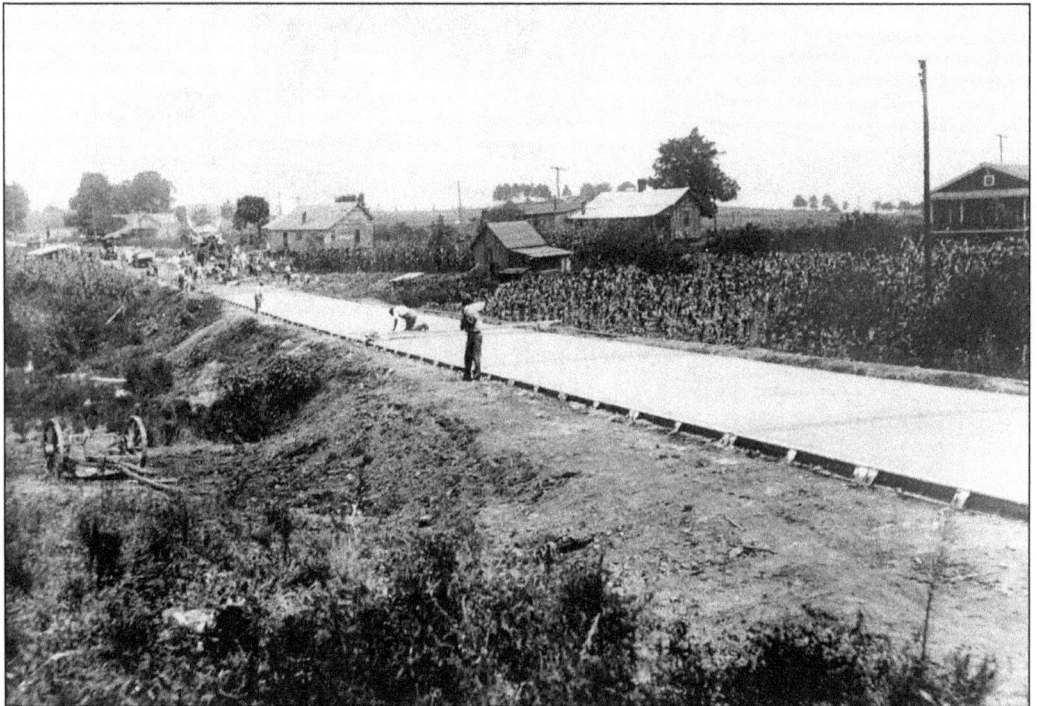

Here concrete has conquered the corn patch as construction of Highway 29 progresses through the county. Farmhouse porches will serve as front-row seats to observe the roaring road.

Two

TIMES ARE CHANGING

A c. 1905 postcard showing the corner of Limestone and Frederick Streets depicts a bustling downtown Gaffney. Today, this intersection is the center of Gaffney's downtown business area. Kimbrells Furniture Store occupies the building in the foreground, and other small family-owned businesses continue in operation.

Shown in a c. 1905 image is Gaffney's City Park, located on Limestone Street. The stately city hall radiates the beauty of Cherokee County. The circle of flowers later became a fountain. On election evenings a huge vote count board was mounted on the north wall of the county courthouse, direcetly across from the park, so townspeople would know the results of the election. The local political stump meetings were moved from the depot to the city hall and park areas.

The Cherokee Drug Company is shown *c.* 1910 at the corner of Frederick and Limestone Streets. It was owned by Dr. Joe Littlejohn, who is seen at right in the doorway, and Dr. Charles Jefferies. In 1944–1945 it became the Merchants and Planters Bank. In 1994, the offices of the *Cherokee Chronicle* were located in this building.

The original Merchant and Planters Bank building was located on the corners of Frederick and Limestone Streets in Gaffney. The bank was created by the merger of two banks in 1887 by banker A.N. Wood. It was federalized on November 11, 1914. In 1969, M&P Bank was absorbed by the Citizens and Southern National Bank. Today it is E.H. Jones Jewelers.

Looking north, this postcard shows the downtown crossroads of Frederick and Limestone Streets in Gaffney. The Merchant and Planters Bank building can be seen on the left. Also visible is the First National Bank on the right with its beautiful marble columns. This is the original financial district of the city.

This 1950s view south from one of the main intersections of town—where Frederick and North Limestone Streets meet—shows Belk's, Leeds Drugs, Rexall, and Graham Cash Company on the left side of the street, and Elgin Watches (right) at E.H. Jones Jewelers. The mall areas have claimed some of these businesses, but others have moved into the buildings after a revitalization project in recent years.

Leander Baker, Ed. H. DeCamp, and A.N. Wood built Gaffney's vaudeville opera house theatre, "The Star," on the corner of Limestone and Birnie Streets. This image shows the theater c. 1902. The first performance, "A Colonial Girl," starred Bertha Creighton and took place on on October 2, 1902. The stage play "Birth of a Nation" and several Shakespeare dramas were well attended. The Star featured stage shows, silent movies, and later, sound movies.

This image of the Baker Building at the corner of Birnie and Limestone Streets in Gaffney is dated around the time of World War I. This building has been a post office, Becham's Mercantile, the Blue Bird Soda Shop, and Middlebrooks Shoe Store. On June 20, 1990, a fire destroyed the structure. L. Baker built a number of the downtown Gaffney buildings. The half-diamond structure atop the building was notable on all L. Baker buildings.

Copeland and Company Building housed the first bank in Gaffney to occupy a brick structure. Built in 1890, the building was located on North Granard and Robinson Streets in Gaffney. Gaffney Bank was on the left, the Copeland Company Hardware was in the center, and I.M. and W. A. Peeler Grocery was on the right.

The intersection of North Granard and West Frederick Streets in Gaffney was home to the old post office, Copeland and Company, the Tin Building (which was a furniture store), and the Shook boarding house at the end of the street. This business area at times included the A.L. Curtis Grocery, Harris Grocery, Col. Sam Jefferies Meat Market, C.B. Poole Wholesale, J.A. Carroll Grocery, Getty's Lumber Company, and Gaffney Electric Company. The Copeland Building burned on December 19, 1967.

This view shows Blacksburg's Shelby Street. O.R. Osborne's General Merchandise (left) was the last three-story building in Blacksburg. Many wooden structures have been replaced with brick buildings. Blacksburg's downtown is experiencing a revitalization and, with that, growing pains.

Blacksburg School was constructed in 1886 and replaced in 1940. It was located on Highway 29. Blacksburg High School is now located on West Ramseur Street; Blacksburg Elementary is on Hardin Street; and Blacksburg Middle is on London Street.

Locals take a break to pose for a picture in front of the Fontanberry Blacksmith Shop, located on the corner of North Granard and Mills Street. Andy Fontanberry (left) was the owner.

The Carnegie Free Public Library was built in 1914, and currently houses the office of the Cherokee County Administrator. Located on North Limestone Street in Gaffney, it was placed on the National Register of Historic Places in 2001.

The Little Building is pictured c. 1920 as the home of Insurance Trust. The building is located on West Frederick Street in Gaffney. Occupying the building today is a store called the Book Shelf as well as offices and Self's Cafe. John Q. Little owns this property.

Shown here is Rose's 5-10-25 Cent Stores located on North Limestone Street in downtown Gaffney. The building is currently occupied by the Peach Center Ministries, a local non-profit offering assistance to the needy.

Peoples Drug Store on North Limestone Street in Gaffney was organized and owned by Drs. R.C. Garland and Claude Flack. Dr. Garland had an optometry office upstairs. The Gaffney Post Office (left) later moved to a larger, more stately building on the corner of North Granard and West Frederick Streets.

The Gaffney Post office is shown at the corner of West Frederick and North Granard Streets in Gaffney. The previous office was in the business district on North Limestone Street. It is now located on West Floyd Baker Boulevard. This building is currently an auto parts store.

Shelby Street in Blacksburg is pictured c. 1916. Blacksburg was proposed as the county seat, but the decision was made by officials to make Gaffney the county seat.

This photograph shows the buildings along North Limestone Street in Gaffney. They are the Hamrick Theater, Byars Dry Goods Store, the old Lipscombe building (housed Harvey's Market), E.T. Parker's Store, and the Baker Building, which housed the Blue Bird, a favorite ice cream parlor. A number of these downtown buildings were designed to provide spaces for smaller businesses.

Blacksburg's City Hall was built in 1898. It has served as the courthouse, jail, and the Masonic and Eastern Star Lodge. After a recent restoration it today houses the Town of Blacksburg Police Department. It is located in the center of downtown Blacksburg.

Gaffney's original city hall, located downtown, was noted for its beautiful architecture and the town clock, which chimed the hours. The City of Gaffney Fire Department is now at this location.

The photograph shows the Cherokee County Courthouse, c. 1930. Built in 1929 of white stone, this beautiful structure continues to serve as the courthouse. The landscaping was donated by Gladys Coker Fort, wife of former S.C. representative and local attorney Claude Fort.

The Cherokee County Sheriff's Department is seen in a photo taken on the side steps of the county courthouse. From left to right are (front row) Jack Morgan, unidentified, Max Wallace, Jimmie Pettitt, and Mack Jolly; (middle row) Wilmon Wright, Ebb Jefferies, Ted Hoke, Ernest Harrington, and Winfred Horton; (back row) two unidentified, ? Byars, unidentified, and Julian Wright. Wright served as sheriff for many years.

This early photograph of Gaffney's Main Street shows the Gaffney Manufacturing Company smoke stack in the background. Businesses were closed on Sundays and everyone enjoyed a day of rest.

Three

OUR GRAND
OLD LADIES

Dr. S.B. Sherrard's home was located on the corner of Buford and South Granard Streets in Gaffney. Dr. Sherrard built a hospital in 1911 on the corner of Logan and Race Streets called the Second Hospital. The first hospital is on West Robinson Street and is now a private residence. Cherokee County residents are now receiving medical services at its fourth facility, the Upstate Carolina Medical Center.

The Piedmont Springs Mineral Company Hotel was established in 1905 as a summer resort. Guests from North and South Carolina would partake of the "health cure" from the springs while staying at the 44-room hotel, which offered a bowling alley, tennis courts, and a swimming pool. It was destroyed by fire in 1914.

The Nuckolls House in Gaffney, complete with four outside chimneys, is located on Asbury Road. It was constructed c. 1790 and is renowned for the well-crafted spiral staircase in the entrance hall. It was once destroyed by fire and rebuilt around the original chimneys. Congressman John C. Calhoun was once entertained there by Mr. Nuckolls, a successful planter and U.S. Congressman. The home is now owned by Mr. and Mrs. Gene Horne and is listed on the National Register of Historic Places.

Shown here is the Thomson Hotel in Blacksburg. Blacksburg was noted for its fine hotels and mineral springs.

The house, located on the corner of Frederick and Anthony Streets in Gaffney, is a beautiful example of a turn-of-the-century home. Known as the I.Q. Anthony home, it was shared in the pat by the Byrd and Albert Kirby families.

Getty's Hotel in Blacksburg was located near the railroad, making it very convenient for travelers. Blacksburg became a resort area due to its mineral waters and location along the railroad routes, offering a stop-over for travelers.

The Black family, consisting of three brothers for whom the town of Blacksburg was named, lived in this house. Black's Station, as the town was known, was changed to Blacksburg in 1888. The Black brothers played a major role in establishing and building Blacksburg. The brothers were Thomas, William C., and Dr. John Gillard Black. Dr. John G. Black erected this c. 1880 home. The house was constructed of bricks, 24 inches thick. It burned in 1945 and was restored, but in August 1958 it was totally destroyed.

The Thompson Robbs House was constructed c. 1889 of handmade bricks produced on-site. The property included the large home and a carriage house. The spindle work trim is an excellent example of the architecture of the period. Mr. Robbs almost single-handedly constructed one of the finest old mansion-type homes in Cherokee County. It was located on West Buford Street in Gaffney, now the site of the Auto Zone.

Constructed by Edgar Henry Gaines in 1920, this home is located at 405 College Drive and today houses "Jolly Place," a bed-and-breakfast inn. The frame house was built with beautiful rock work trim. Gaffney's Mayor and Mrs. Henry Jolly are the proprieters of the inn.

The Claude Jefferies home on Granard Street in Gaffney was built c. 1896 by Col. Sam Jefferies as a gift to his son. Mr. and Mrs. Jefferies are pictured to the left and the children, from left to right, are Irma, Irene, Elizabeth, Sam, Leonora, and the infant in the nurse's arms is Doris. The home was remodeled extensively and named "Roselawn."

Built around the turn of the century, the beautiful J.O. Little home is located on East Frederick Street in Gaffney. Today, it houses the Shuford Hatcher Funeral Home.

The Johnson Home, located on the corner of Limestone and Montgomery Streets in Gaffney, is presently used as the Chamber of Commerce office. It was constructed of cinder block c. 1900, which was at the time radical and unpopular.

This 1907 photograph shows the H.D. Wheat home on Granard Street in Gaffney. The house was built in 1894.

The Henry Gaffney Home, built in the mid-1800s and located on Highway 11 (West Floyd Baker Boulevard), was listed as the 11th most-threatened property in South Carolina in 2000. Henry Gaffney was the son of Michael Gaffney, founder of the town of Gaffney. The house, known as Meadowbrook, contains wide original plank flooring, beadboard ceilings, and original pillars on the front porch. The home was shelter to many Confederate soldiers due to Mr. Gaffney's belief that you never turn away a tired and hungry soldier. In April 1865 a Confederate lieutenant, delivering a sealed message from Jefferson Davis to Gen. Kirby Smith in Texas, rode from Charlotte, North Carolina to Gaffney's Cross Roads, spending the night at Meadowbrook. Highway construction and commerce severely threatens the house.

The Junius Lipscomb house is pictured here on South Johnson Street in Gaffney, c. 1902. The home is presently occupied by the Lipscombs' daughter, Florence. Large magnolia trees shade the house today.

The Brick House Place was built in the 1700s by John Jefferies using a special brick purchased in England and shipped to Gaffney. The bricks were brought by wagons from Charleston, South Carolina. This was the first two-story brick house in the area and Jefferies was soon nicknamed "Brick House John."

Cherokee Inn.

Blacksburg S.C.

Mr. and Mrs. Scott Brown
Proprietors

An All The Year 'Round Resort.

Malarial Diseases and Hay Fever Unknown.   Mineral Springs Rich
in Medicinal Properties. Sulphur, Lithia, Magnesia, &c.
Accessible by all direct routes.

Cherokee Inn.

Blacksburg S.C.

These two business cards to the left advertise the Cherokee Inn in Blacksburg, which is depicted in the drawing above. This c. 1894 inn was a popular resort because of local mineral springs and the inn was owned by Maj. John F. Jones. In July 1898 the inn was acquired by J.D. Kennedy and D.L. Brown. In 1899 M.M. Freeman purchased the inn. In 1901 it was open under the supervision of Scott Brown and was considered a first-class hotel in Blacksburg. In 1902 John Byars purchased the inn. During the Civil War, the Confederate government used the springs at the inn to manufacture epsom salts. The Lithia Inn and Sulphur Springs Inn along with the Cherokee Inn were summer gathering spots for guests from all over the state. Many banquets, parties, and other social events were held at the Cherokee Inn.

The Hotel Carroll in Gaffney, known for its delicious lemon meringue pie, offered travelers the finest in accommodations. It was constructed in 1921 on North Granard Street. During a dangerous thunderstorm in the 1920s, a plane was forced to land at the local airport and the pilot spent the night at the Hotel Carroll—that pilot was Amelia Earhart. The hotel was destroyed by fire in 1980.

The White House Inn was constructed in 1910 by Edward Cash as a grand Greek Revival home. Operating as a bed and breakfast, the structure was beautifully restored in 1980 by Jim White and sold to Pat and Tony Krysiak. Located at 607 West Pine Street in Blacksburg, the inn offers guests the ultimate experience of Southern hospitality.

The Goudelock House and Cabin are located at the junction of SC Highway 18 and SC Highway 211, about 12 miles south of Gaffney. The house was built *c.* 1810 and the cabin dates prior to the Revolutionary War. Although the house has been renovated from time to time over the years, it still retains much of its original appearance and charm and is currently inhabited by the Goudelock family. Columns of the front porch are original posts of cedar. The fireplace has a hand-carved mantel and the stairway handrail is also hand-carved. The log cabin has since undergone some restoration efforts. Deeds verify the property from a land grant from the King of England, Charles II, because the Goudelock family had supported him in exile. The royal land grant was 2,000 acres.

Four

A WORLD OF LEARNING

Pictured here are students at the Beaverdam School c. 1939. The school, located on Highway 29 South in Gaffney, has been converted into the DeCamp House Restaurant.

"The Dummy Line," a one-track line, was used to deliver stone blocks from the limestone quarry to the Industrial Depot downtown. A passenger car was later added to facilitate transportation for the Limestone College students to the downtown area, c. 1904. The dummy line transported lime from the Limestone Spring Lime Works to the Southern Railway in downtown Gaffney. Mr. J.A. Carroll purchased the passenger cars to carry Limestone College students to and from Gaffney. The quarry was located behind the college.

Summer can't be too far away for these pupils, students from one of the elementary schools in Cherokee County.

Girls at Limestone College pose in front of the fountain. They were members of the National French Horn Club c. 1931.

Female basketball players from Gaffney High School pose in their stylish uniforms for a photograph in 1918.

Shown here are members of the 1917 Gaffney High School football team. Pictured from left to right are (front row) T.P. Turner, Raymond Dobson, Dudley Camp, and Paul Green; (middle row) Leslie McCulloch, Albert Sarratt, Robert Fontenberry, and John Davidson; (back row) Coach Mobley, Bill Badger, Rawley Haas, J.C. Hall, Charlie Powers, George Holtzclaw, and Earl Wilkins.

Graduation day was a time for smiles, memories, and great expectations.

On March 10, 1923 South Carolina governor Thomas McLeod authorized $300,000 for the construction of the Gaffney High School. It was built in two stages between 1924 and 1926. The first graduation ceremonies were held in 1927. It was torn down in 1968 and a new facility was built on the same property, which is now Gaffney Middle School on East Frederick Street.

The picture depicts the old Blacksburg Primary School on West Cherokee Street. After a new school was built this property now houses a church.

STATE LINE SCHOOL BUS-1924

Passengers ride aboard a State Line school bus in 1924. This vehicle was an example of necessity being the mother of invention. The State Line Community in Gaffney did not receive school bus service in 1924 so the students' parents designed and built their own school bus to transport them to school.

The West End school building opened in 1917 after construction by V.I. Spurgeon. Its gothic style was a two-story rectangular plan with extended wings. The concrete panel shield designs were inscribed "Faith, Hope, Charity and Thrift." The building served students in Gaffney for many years before burning in the 1980s.

Another school year begins for these young students. Many small, rural schools were located throughout Cherokee County.

The old Beaverdam school was located on Old Georgia Highway in Gaffney. It is now known as the DeCamp House.

The Boy Scouts of Central School pose for this photograph. The Central School was replaced with a new building in 1954 and remained open until 1998. In 1999 the Cherokee Historical and Preservation Society purchased the property as a future site of the Cherokee County History Museum and Art Center.

GAFFNEY, S. C.
Graded School

The Gaffney Male and Female Seminary, located at College Drive and Johnson Street, is seen as it appeared in 1894. It was originally planned as a boys seminary by W.F. McArthur and R.O. Sams. The building was razed after many renovations. In 1954–1955 a new Central Elementary School was built on the property; it is now the proposed site of the Cherokee County History Museum and Art Center.

Co-education the order of the day. English, Classical, Mathematical and Business.

Bookkeeping a specialty.

Music and Art under the control of efficient teachers.

Offers the same advantages to young ladies as to young men.

Young men and young ladies board in entirely seperate apartments.

Our students easily obtain the best situations.

Terms made reasonable to suit the pressure of the times.

For catalogue and further particulars address either of the principals.

W. F. McARTHUR, } Principals.
R. O. SAMS,

Gorgeous legs . . . and they played basketball, too! This photo was taken at Izaak Walton Park in Gaffney. The original lime kilns at Limestone College were developed into a park with a swimming pool. The pool was contracted May 27, 1923 to be 35 feet by 120 feet wide and 9 feet deep. The pool and park were closed in the 1960s.

Possom Trot School, a one-room school house built in 1880, was restored in 1969. It is located on I-85 South and will be moved to the Cherokee County History Museum and Art Center in Gaffney. Children continue to have classes when they visit the school, which was used as a school until 1909. The desks and furnishings are similar to what might have actually been in the school, including some late 19th-century books. As was common among rural schools of the time, there were no graded classes at Possum Trot.

58

Blacksburg Centralized High School was completed in 1928. It was torn down in the early 1970s and replaced with a more modern facility.

Shown here is the Gaffney High School marching band and its high-stepping majorettes.

Cherokee Normal Industrial Institute was Cherokee County's first state-chartered school for African Americans. It was located on Old Georgia Highway in Gaffney. In the photograph

above, unidentified students pose *c.* 1906 in front of the school. Their attire is a wonderful example of the period clothing.

This undated photograph is of the Sunnyside School. When the older Elm Tree and Sunnyside Schools consolidated in 1912 this was founded as the Sunnyside Grammar and High School. Only a 10th-grade education was required. With the addition of the 11th grade, Sunnyside became an elementary school and the higher grades transferred to the Hickory Grove High School in York, South Carolina. It was closed in 1963.

The Confederate veterans, at the request of Dr. Lee Davis Lodge, had this structure built as a depository for the Confederacy's historical documents and as a school of history. It was named after Winnie Davis, daughter of Confederate president Jefferson Davis. First planned in 1899, it was finally completed by 1904. The Greek Revival masonry style takes advantage of natural light with three full windows to each room. This photo was taken c. 1903.

Five

SUNDAY MEETINGS

Buford Street Methodist Church, located on the corner of East Buford and South Petty Streets in Gaffney, is pictured here, c. 1900.

Everyone looks prim and proper at the Cherokee Avenue Baptist Church in Gaffney. This is believed to be a Fourth of July Celebration. Reverend Kirby is the third from the left. The church is noted for its beautiful beaded glass windows. Their Sunday school started in 1894 in the E.R. Cash home. In 1895 the First Baptist, Providence Baptist, and Limestone Churches met and formally organized the Second Baptist Church (this church). Rev. B.P. Robertson was the first pastor. The basement was once used by Gaffney Manufacturing Company for a free school for its employees' children. In 1901 the name was changed to Cherokee Avenue Baptist Church.

Cherokee Avenue Baptist Church is noted for its fine architecture and beautiful beaded glass windows.

First Baptist Church was built c. 1900. It is located on Limestone Street in downtown Gaffney and boasts of having the tallest steeple in Gaffney. The original church was founded in 1878 at the corner of Smith Street. The present church was constructed in the 1950s and was recently renovated.

Members of the first ladies' Sunday school class at the First Baptist Church attend a class reunion. For this special event the ladies dressed in period attire.

This is an early photo of the county's first Mormon church.

Providence Baptist Church, established in 1802, was rebuilt in 1879. The brick structure has been remodeled and currently has an active church family. The church is located on Providence Road and is the site of the oldest church within the present city limits of Gaffney. This previous site before Providence Church was an Indian Village. Its cemetery dates to the early 1800s, with a number of antebellum tombstones.

This is the Island Creek Baptist Church. It is located on Battleground Road near Cowpens, South Carolina.

Many small community churches dotted the county, offering spiritual support to residents. Sardis United Methodist Church is located on Sardis Road in the McKown's Mountain community of Cherokee County. It remains an active congregation of community residents.

Limestone Street United Methodist Church was enlarged in 1898 and considered a "sightly and commodious house of worship." Today, the building is stone-faced and the tower has been moved to a central location directly in front of the entrance to the church. The church is located on North Limestone Street in Gaffney.

Bethel Baptist Church is located on the corner of Meadow Street and Floyd Baker Boulevard in Gaffney. This picture is from the 1930s before two renovations and additions. Bethel has a large congregation and is very active in community affairs. The church was organized on January 26, 1893 under Rev. Galvin Cash. In 1922, the present-day church was built. The church has completed its fourth addition and renovation to the property.

Mulberry Chapel, built in 1869, was the first church for African Americans in the area. Constructed of clapboards over a log frame, the building was no longer used for services after the 1940s. The grounds were the site of the Littlejohn family reunions. As the building is in need of restoration, the Littlejohn Family Reunion has moved to a local school gymnasium in Gaffney. The original furnishings and benches remain in the church today. The chapel is located on Asbury Road in Gaffney.

Six

Pioneers of Industry

The Victor Ice Plant was established in 1890 as part of the Victor Cotton Oil Company complex, built by June Lipscomb. The Victor Cotton Oil Company was incorporated March 21, 1899. When operating at full capacity, it could gin 9,000 bales of cotton a year. The company sold cotton oil, seed, rice, meal, and fertilizer. The V.C.O. Co. was located on East Frederick Street, now the home of the Gaffney Law Enforcement Center.

Mr. A.W. Goforth, front right, was a pastor and teacher at Limestone Baptist Church. He is pictured with members the Thicketty Mountain Association of Pastors and Church officers at their annual meeting. The Thicketty Mountain Association remains very active in church affairs in Cherokee County.

This youngster is waiting for some good ol' ice cream at the Blue Bird on North Limestone Street. Mrs. Byars and "Chick" Wood were always behind the counter to serve customers. The Blue Bird, famous for shaved ice soft drinks, was located on North Limestone Street in downtown Gaffney.

72

This turn-of-the-century photograph shows Edward R. Cash and his wife. He originally established his family in Gaffney as a member of Gaffney Manufacturing Company's first staff. An entrepreneur, he later established the Globe Manufacturing Company, which eventually failed and was sold. He then moved to Blacksburg and entered the furniture and mercantile business. The Globe Manufacturing Co. on 13th Street as well as Gaffney Manufacturing Company on Railroad Avenue produced textiles fabric. A complete mill village, consisting of homes, company stores, and churches, emerged around the mills.

The Gaffney Fire Department's engine #3 was a 1946 GMC, purchased from Byars-McIntyre Motors. This is an undated photo of the volunteer fire department attached to city hall. Among those standing are Brossie Jones, ? Huffstetler, W.C. "Bub" Burgess, and Fire Chief Dever "Skeeter" Coyle (far right).

Three ladies pose behind the soda fountain in the local drug store in downtown Gaffney. From left to right, they are Virginia Prichard, Grace Vinesett, and Winfra Leigh.

The City Hospital of Gaffney was built by Dr. S.B. Sherrard and located on South Logan Street. This was the second hospital in Gaffney. The fourth hospital, Upstate Carolina Medical, now serves the residents of the county.

A sales meeting of the C.B. Poole Wholesale Company takes place in the early 1940s. Pooles Wholesale was a family-owned business located on North Granard Street in Gaffney.

Mr. Edward Littlejohn was Gaffney's only African-American postmaster until 2002. The post office was located at North Limestone and Birnie Streets in the L. Baker Building in downtown Gaffney.

BROAD RIVER MILLS ABOUT 1918

Broad River Mills, located in Blacksburg, is shown in this *c.* 1918 image. It remained in operation until after World War II. Note the watertank and dwellings that surround the textile mill.

Hiram D. Wheat was originally recruited as a treasurer in 1892 by the Gaffney Manufacturing Company's founding entrepreneurs. He quickly became the CEO and manager. Mr. Wheat was born near Columbia, South Carolina, and began working in a mill at a young age. Despite a limited education, his intelligence brought him quick recognition as an outstanding worker and then supervisor. Soon enough, it was discovered he had an understanding of finances, and this eventually caught the attention of Gaffney Manufacturing Company. Mr. Wheat expanded his philanthropy to the community. He was married to Anna Cannon Wheat and had two children—Irene and Harry. His most generous contribution was a lovely city park named after his daughter Irene. The park's lake, with a gazebo on an island, meandering trails along the water's edge, private gardens, and rental boats and paddle boats are fond memories for Cherokee County residents. The English botanist George James was responsible for the lovely gardens. This wonderful area was drained, filled in, and is now a ball field for the city.

This is a picture of workers at the Sarratt and Sims Company. The architecture of the building is a fine example of stone work in early Gaffney.

This early picture shows what is today known as Broad River Brick Company, located on Victory Trail Road in Gaffney. The Broad River Brick Company was purchased by Boren Clay and today has a modern facility off Interstate–85 north of Gaffney in Blacksburg.

Located on Highway 5 in Blacksburg, the Burton Dixie Company is seen as it appeared in earlier times. Opened in 1929 by two Chicago gentlemen, Mr. Burton and Mr. Dixie, the mill produced cotton and springs used in bed springs and chair cushions. The metal springs division continues in operation today.

This aerial view shows the Limestone Mill and the adjacent mill village in Gaffney. Textiles have always been a major industry in Cherokee County and these villages were a community unto itself.

Gaffney Manufacturing Company kept sheep on their lawns. Many locals remember the sheep wandering the grounds and keeping the grass "mowed." Located on Railroad Avenue in Gaffney, the mill was built in 1892. The initial "financial subscription" of $10,000 was made by Mr. J.A. Carroll. The plant was purchased by the Milliken group and ceased operation in 2000. The trees are ginkos, which offer a golden view in fall.

H. D. WHEAT
PREST & TREAS.

The Irene Mills

MANUFACTURERS AND FINISHERS OF
DAMASK NAPKINS AND TOWELS

JAMES F. WHITE & CO., Inc.
54 WORTH ST., N.Y.
SELLING AGENTS

Gaffney S.C.

This is a card from the Irene Mills in Gaffney. Established by H.D. Wheat, the mill was named after his daughter Irene. The popular Irene Park was located on the mill property.

Gaffney Manufacturing Company and Cotton Market was built in 1892 and financed by a group of men organized by J.A. Carroll. The business remained in operation until 2000. The mill was located at North Limestone Street and Railroad Avenue adjacent to the downtown business district of Gaffney.

A postcard depicting Gaffney's Cotton Market says that 600 bales of cotton were sold on October 16, 1919, at 35¢ a pound.

Becker's Bakery and Gaffney's Filling Station, located on the corner of North Limestone and Meadow Streets in Gaffney, were prosperous downtown enterprises *c.* 1937. Becker's Bakery, which dates from 1907, later moved to Robinson Street. Becker's claim was "the health balancer of the community I serve." This included "cream bread" and "for dessert on every occasion may we suggest Virginia Dare cake. We will always foster the advanced for the HEALTH-UP BUILDING of our friends and neighborhoods."

The Settlemeyer Building was nicknamed "hole in the wall" due to the corner-notched opening on the third floor. This three-story brick building is pictured on the corner of North Limestone and Robinson Streets in Gaffney c. 1904. The building has been renovated as an apartment house. The small building to the left is the Freight Depot for the City of Gaffney; it has been razed. The brownstone and marble used on the front of the Settlemeyer Building was new to Gaffney. It housed many businesses, including Southern Express Co., Gaffney Drug Co., Western Union Telegraph, and Savings and Loan Co.

This photograph shows the interior of one of the many banks ready to provide services for local businesses in Gaffney.

Foster's Funeral Home, established in 1919, is located on North Petty and Meadow Streets in Gaffney. Rufus Foster Sr. was the owner, and it is operated today by Rufus Foster Jr. Foster's has a new building today next to the original facility. (Photo courtesy of Rufus Foster Jr. and James Goforth.)

Standing in front of the Gordon-Harrison Mortuary in Blacksburg, from left to right, are Johnny Hopper, J.D. Harrison, Bill Gordon, ? Mabry, Roy Harrison, and unidentified.

This Standard Gasoline and Motor Oil Co. service station was located on North Granard Street in Gaffney and is now occupied by Petty Tire Company. At the front pump stands W.L. Vassy. The Cook family home is to the right; the site of what once boasted this beautiful Victorian home is now a parking lot.

Campbell Limestone Quarry, located to the rear of Limestone College, was re-opened in 1932 by R.S. Campbell Sr. It produced crushed aggregate for road-building and lime for agricultural purposes. A slab of limestone from this quarry is South Carolina's contribution to the Washington Monument in Washington, D.C. In 1954, the company moved to Blacksburg and later merged with Vulcan Materials Inc. R.S. Campbell Jr. assumed the presidency of the company upon the death of his father. Limestone and marble were mined at this site as early as 1820. The quarry later became the source of limestone flux for the iron industries in Cherokee County.

These three original kilns were located behind Limestone College. They were removed when the quarry was enlarged after World War II.

A 1946 Chevrolet truck waits at the scale at the Limestone Quarry in Gaffney.

GRIT AND STEEL

PUBLISHED IN THE INTEREST OF THOSE DEVOTED TO THE GAME FOWL.

Vol. I.　　　GAFFNEY, S. C., MAY, 1899.　　　No. 1.

CONTENTS.

Grit and Steel is a magazine that has been published in Cherokee County continually for 103 years. It focuses on the raising of game-fowl, which is legal in the state of South Carolina, even though cock-fighting is illegal. The magazine is one of three such publications world wide.

Seven

FROM TROTTING
TO TREADING

A wholesaler offers free ginger ale samples to locals gathered in front of the Gaffney Drug Company. At the time this image was taken, horses and buggies were used to carry goods, such as drinks, to different businesses in a variety of towns. The photo was taken in front of the Settlemeyer Building on North Limestone Street in Gaffney.

Riding into town on an ox-pulled cart was not an unusual sight during the time when this photograph was taken *c.* 1900.

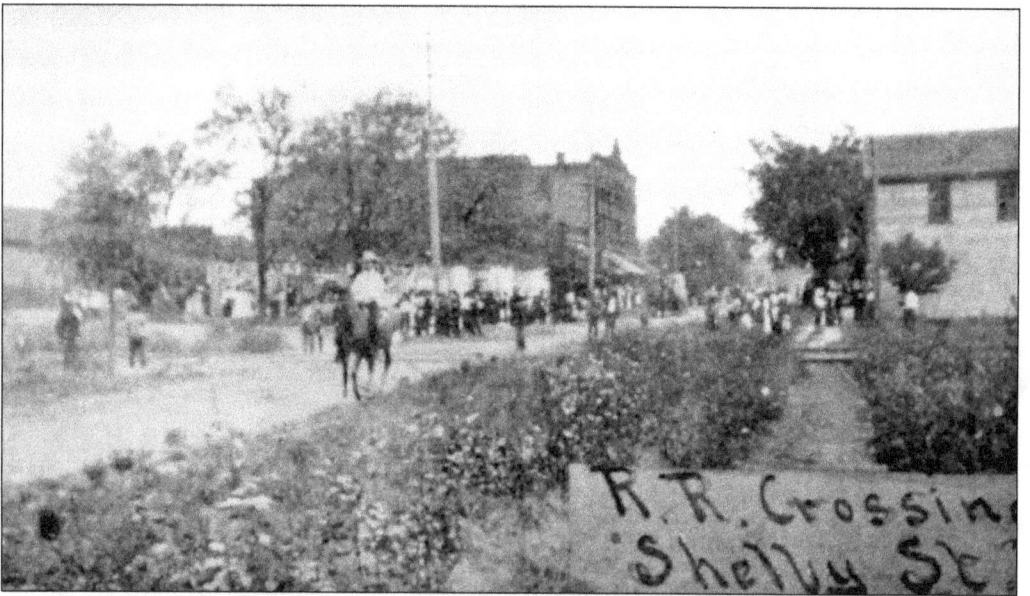

This photograph shows the Blacksburg railroad crossing on Shelby Street looking toward the intersection of what is today S.C. Highway 29. The imposing three-story structure (left) is O.R. Osborne General Merchandise at the end of the 19th century. In 1916, a fire destroyed much of the downtown area and there has been no three-story building since in Blacksburg.

The workers in this photograph were constructing Highway 29, a national roadway extending from New Orleans to New York, near Cherokee Creek. The grading is being done by a mule-drawn "drag-pan."

On the right is the "new" 1918 railroad trestle over Thicketty Creek. The old trestle, center, is being converted into a bridge for SC Highway 29. The old Highway 29 bridge, left, was the tallest highway bridge in the state at this time.

Norfolk Southern Railway No. 1218 steam train crosses Thicketty Creek bridge.

These people are waiting for a train in Blacksburg.

This postcard depicts the Southern Railroad Depot in Gaffney c. 1908. Located only one block from the business district of Gaffney, the depot was a busy integral part of our early history. The depot was razed and replaced with a parking lot.

A political rally is held at the Gaffney Depot. These local political rallies were a common event which were later moved uptown at the City Park and Agriculture Building in North Limestone Street in Gaffney.

The Irene Garage was a public garage owned by H.D. Wheat. Located on the corner of Buford and Logan Streets in Gaffney, it was destroyed by a tornado in the 1930s. The garage was located behind the Wheat mansion facing Logan Street and named for Wheat's daughter. Because of repeated breakdowns of his car, Mr. Wheat hired and paid for a permanent mechanic. It is thought each of these cars belonged to a member of his family even though this was a public garage.

A *c.* 1912 photograph reveals the interior of The Irene Garage in Gaffney. Mr. Badger and his three sons were the mechanics for the Irene Garage.

H.D. Wheat was the first car owner in Gaffney. His "Pierce Arrow" was very impressive.

This unusual view displays an early truck, which belonged to Raymond Parker's dad, in motion. The image was taken by suspending a camera from the barrel of a gun and moving right to left with the motion of the vehicle. The sign on the side of the truck reads "Bubbly" soft drink. It was undoubtedly taken in the early 20th century.

These vintage 1930 school buses were the new models used to transport Gaffney High School students.

96

Built *c.* 1919, The Gaffney T-Bridge is on West Montgomery Street. Gaffney crosses the Southern Railway tracks. There are only a few other bridges of this shape left in the world. The bridge allows traffic access after the tracks when trains are present. Jefferies House, built in 1884, is the best example of the residential Italianate style in Gaffney. Today it is the home of White Columns Funeral Home.

The Junior Chamber of Commerce held a "safe driving campaign." Included in the photograph are Bill Martin, E.H. Jones, and Billy Hatcher Sr.

A billboard greets people arriving at South Carolina's border, reminding them to drive safely. How appropriate to have a safe driving campaign with not-so-common snow on the ground. This was part of the Junior Chamber of Commerce safe driving campaign.

Couples could fly in the plane and be married by Lake Stroupe, a probate judge. In 1927, from left to right, a pilot, two witnesses, the couple, Lake Stroupe, and Sam Littlejohn wait in front of the airplane on the Hamrick Golf Course (Limestone Street). The plane is Ford Tri-Motor style.

Eight

BACK ROADS, BRIDGES, AND BEATEN PATHS

The mighty Broad River provided food, transportation, and recreation to Cherokee County residents. Today, 17 miles of the river have been designated as Scenic River.

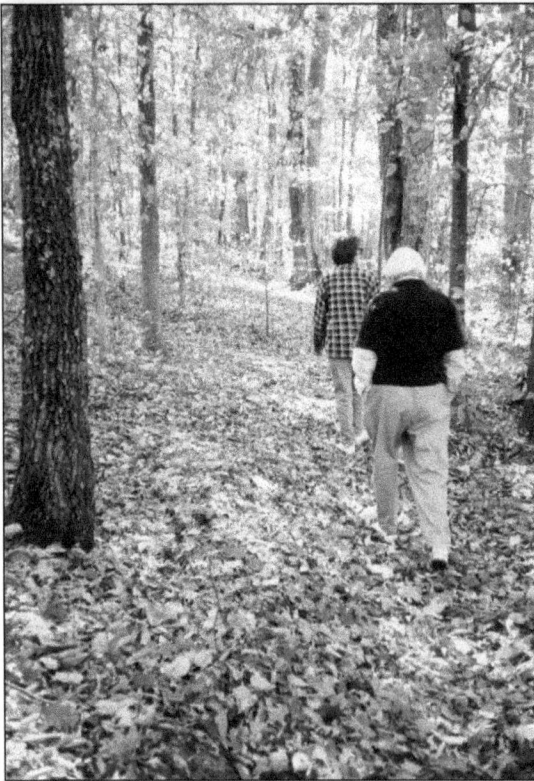

Another part of the Overmountain Victory Trail around Lake Whelchel in Gaffney makes for long, quiet walks. The Overmountain Victory Trail is part of the National Historic Trail System. The OVT Historic Trail begins in Abingdon, Virginia and continues 220 miles to King's Mountain Military Park. March reenactors gather in Abingdon and follow the route of assembly of the American Patriot Army, which decisively defeated an American loyalist army at the Battle of King's Mountain in the fall of 1780. Here, Emmie Rector and C.J. enjoy the trail.

Cherokee Ford on the Broad River is a segment of the Overmountain Victory National Historic Trail. It is here that the militia crossed on their way to the battle of Kings Mountain during the American Revolution, 1780. After resting on October 6 at Cowpens, the militia continued in pursuit of Ferguson's Army. On October 7, the Patriot Army crossed the Broad River at Cherokee Ford. At 3 p.m. the same day, the Patriots found Ferguson's Loyalist Army at at King's Mountain. The crossing was declared a historic site in October 2000.

The Dravo Bridge in Blacksburg was the only curved bridge in the county. The bridge crossed two springs that emptied into the Broad River.

The fountain at City Park in Gaffney is surrounded by beautiful, hand-made wrought iron.

Many lazy afternoons were spent at Irene Park, built by Mr. H.D. Wheat. The young lady to the left of this c. 1907 image is believed to be the builder's daughter, Irene Wheat. Stella Jefferies, Jim Byars, and Jim Nesbitt join in the fun at the lake.

This picture shows the Irene Mill and Irene Park area.

Grist mills were commonplace in Cherokee County. Referred to as Sprooger's Mill, this mill is located on Little Thicketty Creek.

Furnace Mill and Waterwheel is located at Furnace Mountain, off the scenic Highway 11. The area is known as the Furnace Place, but was once known as Nesbitt's Furnace—a Revolutionary War ironworks. The original wooden wheel was replaced by the present iron wheel. The wheel turned by the waterflow and county residents brought their corn and wheat there to be ground. The mill closed in the late 1950s or early 1960s, and the mill itself was eventually destroyed by fire. Restoration of the area has begun and the landmark is a stop on the Overmountain Victory Trail march. The property was donated to the county by the family of Gladden Smoak in 2000.

Although water no longer flows, the old water-wheel remains as a testament to by-gone days of production.

Nine

SOUTHERN PASTIMES

The granddaughter of H.D. Wheat, Anna Wheat Richardson (left), visits with her best friend Stella Jefferies in the solarium of the Wheat home.

An early-1900s photographer's studio is a portrait of days gone by. Located in downtown Gaffney, this is believed to be the Tuttle Studio.

Local children and teenagers wait in line for entrance to the matinee at the Cherokee Theater in Gaffney. The marquee promotes *The Fighting Chance*, starring Rod Cameron.

The Small Fry Café, located on Cherokee Avenue near the railroad, sold candy and hot dogs. The Small Fry Gang, a group of friends who patronized the location for years, offers scholarships to graduating seniors from Gaffney Senior High and Blacksburg High School.

Patrons of the Small Fry Cafe are pictured *c.* 1940 enjoying time with their friends at the local watering hole and hangout.

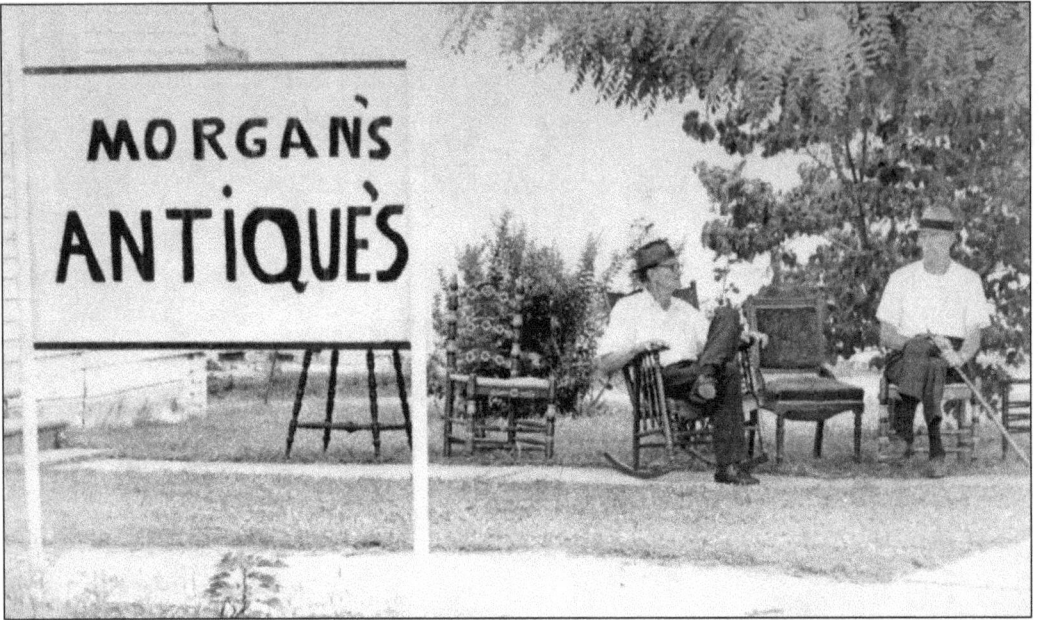

Mr. James Morgan's antique shop was located on Cherokee Avenue. Mr. Morgan and Mr. Eddie Russell Parker sitting outside the shop—weather permitting—and visiting with friends and customers was a familiar sight for Gaffney residents.

Irma Jefferies and Horace Lister Bass Jr. were married on June 29, 1929. Noted photographer June Carr took this image on the porch of the bride's mother, Lizzie Fort Jefferies. The wedding party included members of Gaffney's first families.

The Strand Theater on North Limestone Street offered hours of escape to various fantasy worlds. Gloria Swanson was always sure to draw a crowd. The Strand Theater was built in 1903.

The male members of the band, from right to left, are Howard Pegram, Bernard Harvey, and Steedley Cook. The female members are unidentified.

Bird hunting always provided fresh air, fun, and good company in Cherokee County. Originally a private home, this old building was later used as a hunting cabin.

This old chain swing was a part of beautiful Irene Park and was a popular pastime. Those who can be recognized include Winnie Jones Cline, Jesse Jones Plummer, Horace Brown, and Boyd Soloman. This rare photo was provided by Albert Cline.

A Business and Professional Women's Club campaign persuaded people to register to vote.

Weekly checker games took place at the "Big Mill" Community House in Gaffney. The Gaffney Manufacturing Company was known as the Big Mill. This photograph, taken by Rodger Painter, shows Mr. Ed Bridges (left) enjoying a game.

May Day Festivities were held at Limestone College in the early 1900s.

R.L. Wylie, 90, sits in his favorite rocker and looks over his Rock Springs community homeplace.

Stopping only for a moment, Clara Robbs, wife of Felix Robbs, was tending her dahlias at her home on North Logan and West Buford Streets when Rodger Painter photographed her.

Mrs. Wheat was an avid contributor to local causes and a respected member of the community. She is pictured here with her beloved dogs.

The vine-adorned arbor hangs over an intricate brick colonnade at the home of H.D. Wheat on Granard Street. Such gardens were attributed to George James, an English botanist hired by Mr. Wheat to design the gardens on the estate.

Pictured *c.* 1909 is Dorris Jefferies, daughter of James Claude Jefferies and Lizzie Walker Fort Jefferies. She was the mother of Charles Farriss, who worked diligently to provide pictures and information for this book. This photo is from a family album.

Mary Spencer is still able to read the Bible at 100 years of age—without glasses. This photo was taken by Rodger Painter in 1972.

The Jefferies family, photographed on June 30, 1910, includes, from left to right, (front row) Irma and Irene; (back row) Elizabeth, Leonora, and Samuel. This photo, made at the first birthday part of Dorris Jefferies. is from the Charles Farriss Collection.

115

Irene and Harry Wheat are pictured here as children riding in a pony-cart for a May Day celebration. This photo was taken in the early 1900s in front of the Wheat Home on South Granard Street in Gaffney.

This rare, old photo of the Gist brothers is a true treasure. The vest and watch chain worn by the gentleman on the right in the front row shows great style.

Charles Farriss is photographed with his puppy in 1939. Charles's later dedication and hard work was instrumental in the publication of this book. Cherokee County is grateful for his efforts in preserving the area's rich history through photographs.

Coordination of the eyes, hands, and feet are necessary to operate this peddle sewing machine. This photo of Nancy Lee Sellars is by Rodger Painter.

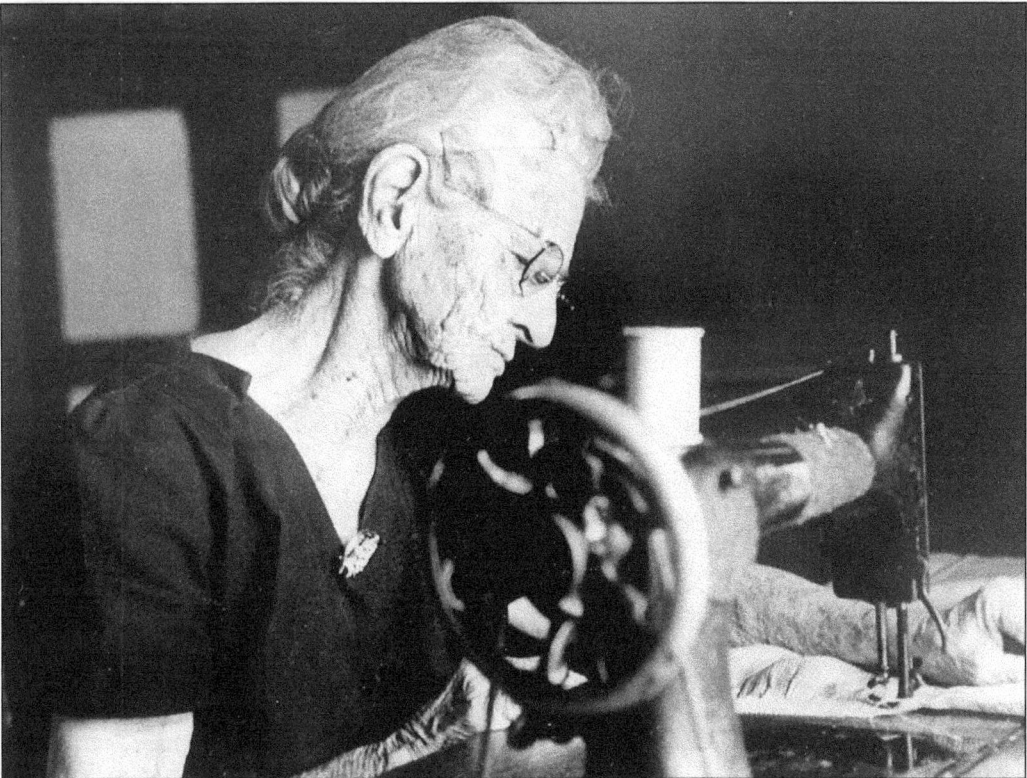

Here one generation helps and learns from the other. Rosa McGill's nimble fingers work to complete a handmade quilt stretched on a frame. Her grandson offers help, but it appears that the needle may have been too much for him. This photo is by Rodger Painter.

These tiny tots are interested in the audience as well as the winner's cup.

A man poses here to show off his T-Model Ford and beautiful daughter. The people in this early 1900s photograph are unidentified.

At the Bell family reunion held at the homeplace, many families in Cherokee County share family gatherings outside to enjoy food, family, and Sunday afternoons.

Mr. J.S. Westmoreland proudly shows off his 1907 Oldsmobile. Friends include Ila Westmoreland, Jasper Peeler, and his sister Miss Holman. This was Cherokee County's third automobile. Mr. Westmoreland wears the proper motoring clothing and appears to have also worn them hunting as well because his bag holds birds.

Ten

FOR FREEDOM
AND COUNTRY

Located near Thicketty Creek, Fort Anderson—better known as "Fort Thicketty"—was built by the British during the American Revolution as a refuge against the Cherokee and Creek Indians. A block house type construction, it is almost square and although in poor condition, still standing. During the Revolutionary War, it was used by Tories for raids against families and farms that were left vulnerable with their men fighting elsewhere. On July 29, 1780, 600 men from Col. Thomas Sumter's command reached the fort and surrounded it by the next morning. British commander Col. Patrick Moore soon surrendered. As Colonel Ferguson approached the fort, he learned of the surrender and turned towards Charlotte and safety with General Cornwallis. En route, he camped at King's Mountain and was killed in the ensuing battle.

Gen. Daniel Morgan's troops defeated the British forces on January 17, 1781, where this monument stands at Cowpens National Battlefield. This battle was the beginning of the end of the American Revolutionary War. On this field, American troops under Brig. Gen. Daniel Morgan won a single victory over a British force commanded by Lt. Col. Banastre Tarleton on January 17, 1781.

The Battles of Kings Mountain and Cowpens are reenacted by volunteers with Revolutionary rifles and equipment (or carefully crafted reproductions). Shown are two modern examples of how the American Mountain Men appeared out on the battlefield.

Upon arrival at Cowpens National Battlefield, some marches have been following the Overmountain Victory Trail from Abingdon, Virginia on their way to King's Mountain National Military Park for a wreath-laying ceremony to honor the heroes of the American Revolution.

123

The Battle of King's Mountain was fatal for South Carolina patriot Col. James Williams on October 7, 1780. He was interred near the Broad River on the Mintz farm, but local citizens later sought to find him a more distinguished burial site. His remains were exhumed in 1911 and stored in the B.A. Holmes store until October 15, 1915, when he was reburied on the Carnegie Library grounds. This picture shows the reburial ceremony on October 8, 1915. The building is now the Cherokee County Administration Office, located on North Limestone Street in Gaffney.

Col. Sam Jefferies regularly attended notable out-of-state performances by actors and actresses. This picture was taken of him prior to attending a performance in New Orleans. Colonel Sam is remembered for his love of horses. Before the War Between the States, he traveled to Tennessee to purchase a foal, the grandson of the famous racehorse, Lexington.

This picture shows Confederate Veterans from Cherokee County. The photo shows a small remnant of the 1,400 local men who served in the Confederate services. Many of Cherokee County's oldest family names are represented.

The Moses Wood chapter of the United Daughters of the Confederacy ordered this statue from Florence, Italy. The marble statue arrived in Gaffney in 1922. It sits atop North Carolina granite. The dedication of the monument was held on May 23, 1923, on Confederate Memorial Day. The Capt. Moses Wood Camp #125 Sons of Confederate Veterans continue the annual Memorial Day services at the monument. The Confederate Memorial Statue is located on the corner of Buford and South Limestone Streets. This photograph was taken by Kent Williams.

The Blacksburg Town Hall, constructed in 1898, has served many purposes over the years: city hall, courthouse, jail, volunteer fire department, Masonic and Eastern Star Lodge, and the mayor's office. This Fourth of July photograph is possibly the very first of the building. Notice that the streets are unpaved.

Gaffney's City Hall is festooned with patriotic flags for a Fourth of July celebration. Also, notice the new appearance of telephone poles with their intruding power lines. This building, as well as the courthouse, was once an opera house with a stage in the front where road shows were performed. The advent of movies brought this to an end.

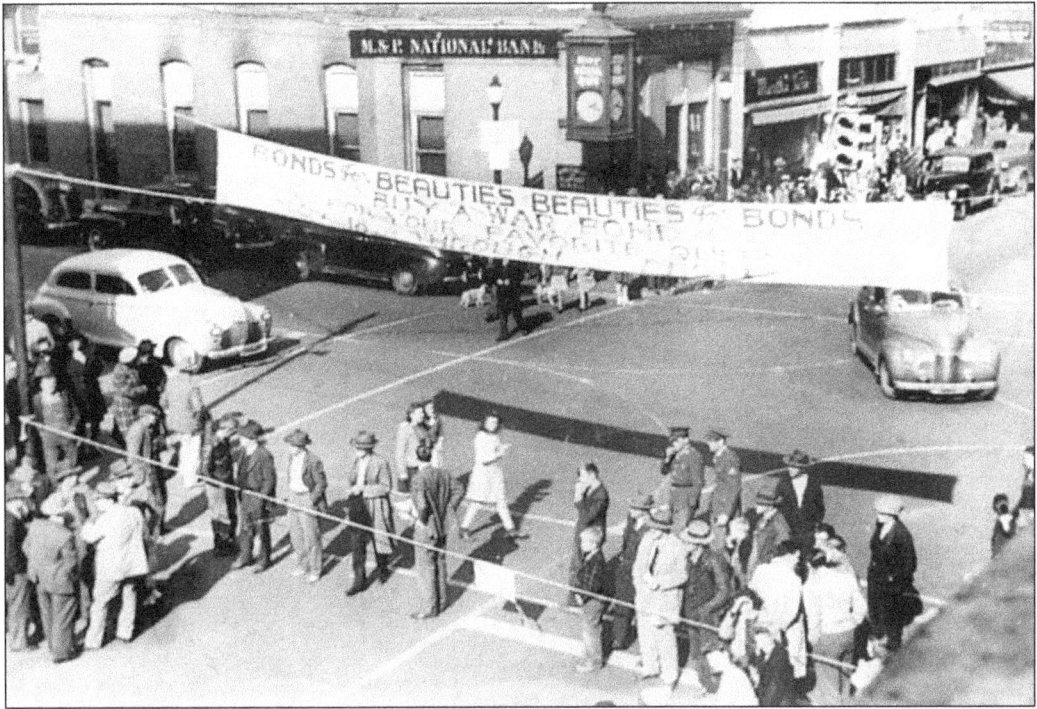

"Bonds for Beauties, Beauties for Bonds" was one way the locals supported the war effort. The banner hangs at the intersection of North Limestone and Frederick Streets in Gaffney.

Pictured is Rufus H. Foster Sr. with the State American Legion Commander. Mr. Foster is being presented with a service recognition award. This photo was provided by Rufus Foster Jr. and James Goforth.

This is a picture of the Auxiliary Police Ward 3-Unit, defenders of the neighborhood. The officers were part of the Home Guards for Gaffney.

Visit us at
arcadiapublishing.com